John Bunyan, Eliza Eberle

The way to the cross: Set forth in rhyming verses

Founded upon the allegorical representations of Bunyan

John Bunyan, Eliza Eberle

The way to the cross: Set forth in rhyming verses
Founded upon the allegorical representations of Bunyan

ISBN/EAN: 9783337257231

Printed in Europe, USA, Canada, Australia, Japan

Cover: Foto ©Andreas Hilbeck / pixelio.de

More available books at **www.hansebooks.com**

THE

WAY TO THE CROSS

Set forth in Rhyming Verses,

FOUNDED UPON THE

ALLEGORICAL REPRESENTATIONS OF BUNYAN.

BY

Mrs. ELIZA EBERLE.

———————

PHILADELPHIA:

PUBLISHED BY JOHN J. EBERLE.

1868.

STEREOTYPED BY
MACKELLAR, SMITHS & JORDAN,
PHILADELPHIA.

THE

WAY TO THE CROSS.

WHILE walking through this wilderness,
    To seek my crown, it seemed
I lighted on a certain den,
    In which I slept and dreamed.

I saw a man all clothed in rags,
    And they were filthy, too,
Not fit to stand before the king
    With whom he had to do.

A burden, too, was on his back,
    Which pressed him with its weight;
Just like a cart beneath its sheaves,
    The burden was so great.

His face was now turned from his house,
    And in his hand a book,
And on the things he once so loved
    He now did shun to look.

3

I saw him reading in his book,
　All trembling and afraid;
Then, with a cry of loud lament,
　"What shall I do?" he said.

In this sad plight, the man went home,
　There sought to be resigned,
That neither wife nor child might know
　The troubles of his mind.

But silence he could not endure,
　And thus I heard him say,
As he to wife and children spake
　In this affecting way:

"Oh, my dear wife with whom I live,
　And children that I love,
A heavy burden lies on me,
　Which I cannot remove:

"Moreover, I have been informed,
　God will this city burn;
This very place wherein we dwell,
　He will to ashes turn.

"And you, my wife, and our sweet babes,
　This judgment will o'ertake,
Unless some way may yet be found
　Whereby we may escape."

At this his friends were much amazed;
　Not that they thought 'twas true,
But feared some frenzy ailed his brain,
　That would his mind undo.

And they, as night was drawing nigh,
  Besought him to repose,
In the vain hope that softening sleep
  Would gently soothe his woes.

But sleep refused to lend her aid
  In banishing his fears,
And all that long and troublous night
  He spent in sighs and tears.

Now, when the morning light was come,
  They asked him how he was:
He told them he was worse and worse,
  And then explained the cause.

But as he talked they harshly chid;
  Their hearts had harder grown;
They thought to drive his gloom away
  By much unkindness shown.

Wherefore he then withdrew himself
  To a secluded place,
And breathed a fervent prayer to God
  To give them saving grace.

Sometimes he read, sometimes he prayed,
  And sometimes walked the fields,
Still seeking for that pearl of price
  Which God to man reveals.

Now, as he read, his fears increased,
  His griefs they stronger grew;
He cried, as he had done before,
  "Lord, save! what shall I do?"

His eyes then wandered here and there,
　　As if he sought to run :
He dreamed not of that blessed path
　　To Thee, Eternal One.

Then one Evangelist drew near,
　　Who said, "Why dost thou cry?"
The man, with trembling heart, replied,
　　"I am condemned to die.

"I have been reading in a book,
　　The book that's in my hand ;
It tells me of a judgment-bar
　　At which I fear to stand.

"My soul will not consent to death ;
　　Judgment I cannot bear ;
The thought falls heavy on my heart,
　　Must I be summoned there?"

Evangelist then made reply,
　　"O man, dost thou suppose
That death makes man's condition worse,
　　Since life is full of woes?"

He answered, "Sir, I am afraid
　　It will be worse with me,
Because this burden on my back
　　Will seal my misery.

" 'Twill sink me lower than the grave,
　　Where devils clank their chains,
And bind me in that doleful cell
　　Where death eternal reigns.

"The things of judgment and of death
   Are placed before mine eye:
I feel so unprepared for them
   That these things make me cry."

Evangelist then said to him,
   "Why then stand still? Oh, fly!
'Tis sure destruction to remain:
   Why wilt thou stay to die?"

He answered, "Darkness reigns around;
   Here thorns and brambles grow:
Alas! the way is new to me;
   I know not where to go."

Evangelist gave him a roll,
   With these words written on:
"Now is the time; escape for life;
   Flee from the wrath to come."

The man then read the parchment roll,
   And, with an anxious sigh,
Looked steady on Evangelist,
   Saying, "Whither shall I fly?"

Evangelist, then, pointing to
   A little narrow gate,
Said, "Run; but turn to neither side,
   Because the way is straight."

He said, "I cannot see the gate,
   Because of yonder field;
But I will try to find the way
   Before my doom is sealed."

Evangelist then asked him if
  He saw "yon shining light,
Lit up for those who pass this way,
  To guide their steps aright."

He answered thus : " I think I see
  A gleaming from afar,
Just like a single shining spark,
  Or like a rising star."

Evangelist then said to him,
  "That light keép still in view,
And thou shalt plainly see the gate
  When thou art up thereto.

"And when thou at the gate hast knocked,
  Thy duty will be plain ;
For one will tell thee what to do,
  Who can these things explain."

Now, in my dream I saw that when
  Evangelist was done,
The man with new encouragement
  Set out with speed to run.

His wife and children saw him run,
  Before he had gone far:
They then cried after him, " Return !
  How very strange you are !"

But on he ran, and cried aloud,
  " Life ! life ! eternal life !"
And put his fingers in his ears,
  And hearkened not to wife.

The neighbors came to see the man,
   As he was on the run;
Some threatened him, while others mocked,
   And others cried, " Return !"

Among these neighbors there were two
   Who thought to take this course :—
" He must come back to us again;
   We'll bring him back by force."

The names of these two wicked men
   Did suit their cases well:
The name of one was Obstinate,
   The other's, Pliable.

Now, by this time the man had gone
   Almost beyond their sight;
But soon these men caught up to him,
   By running with their might.

When they came up, the man then said,
   " Why, neighbors, are ye come?"
They answered him, " To take you back
   To our own native home."

The man replied, " This cannot be;
   By no means I'll return;
Your city is Destruction, sirs;
   It will to ashes burn.

" And all who die there, I am told,
   Sink lower than the grave,
Into a lake of brimstone fire,
   Where none can ever save.

"Oh, then, dear neighbors, be content,
    And come along with me:
Your city is a fearful place,
    I have been made to see."

Said Obstinate, "What! leave our friends
    And comforts all behind?
I never will do this, I'm sure,
    Unless I change my mind."

"All you forsake, then," Christian said,
    (For Christian was his name,)
"Cannot be worthy to compare
    With what will be your gain.

"If you will come along with me,
    You like myself shall share:
I'm going where there is enough,
    And also some to spare."

Said Obstinate, "What are the things
    You leave your all to find,—
The things you think outvalue all
    That you must leave behind?"

"I seek a treasure," Christian said,
    "That fadeth not away,
Laid up in heaven,—not on earth,
    Where all things must decay.

"This treasure is bestowed on all
    Who diligently seek,—
The broken heart, the contrite ones,
    The penitent, the meek.

"I will now for the truth of this
　　Refer you to my book.
Here you can read what I have said:
　　Be wise, and in it look."

"Your book away!" said Obstinate;
　　"What for your book care I?
Will you go back with us, or not,
　　Or still go on, and die?"

Said Christian, "I will not go back,
　　Nor dare I look back now:
I have my face set Zion-ward,
　　My hands put to the plough."

Said Obstinate to Pliable,
　　"It's time we start for home:
If he will not go back with us,
　　We'll let the fool alone.

"Some men, when they get hold upon
　　A thing that doth them please,
Know more, they think, than seven men
　　Who can a reason give."

Said Pliable, "Do not revile:
　　If what he says be true,
He looks, no doubt, for better things
　　Than either I or you.

"I feel inclined to go with him,
　　That unseen coast explore;
I may find solid treasures there,
　　When landed on the shore."

Said Obstinate to Pliable,
  "What! are there more fools still?
Who knows where he would lead you to,
  If you obey his will?"

Said Christian, "Neighbor Pliable,
  Come go along with me;
The things that I have told you of
  You certainly shall see.

"Things far more glorious you shall have
  Than you can now conceive.
This is recorded in my book:
  Do only now believe.

"The promise of these glorious things
  Has been confirmed by blood,—
The precious blood of Jesus slain,
  The only Son of God."

Said Pliable to Obstinate,
  "I think I will decide
To go along with this good man,
  If he will be my guide."

Said Christian, "I am not the guide;
  Evangelist, I say,
Will guide us to that little gate,
  Where pilgrims learn the way."

Then Pliable to Christian said,
  "Come, let us journey on;
My lot is now cast in with yours,
  Our prospects shall be one."

But Obstinate then said to them,
"I will go back again:
I will not keep companionship
With such misguided men."

Then Christian said to Pliable,
"I'm glad you make this choice,
To go with me and prove my words;
It makes my heart rejoice.

"Had even Obstinate himself
Viewed things unseen as we,
He would not thus have turned about
And left our company."

Said Pliable, "Since none are here,
Our speaking to annoy,
Tell me still further of the things
That we shall there enjoy."

Then Christian said to Pliable,
"A subject of this kind
Cannot be spoken by my tongue
As it is in my mind.

"But you can read it in my book,
If you desire to know:
'Tis it I get my knowledge from,
To it I daily go."

Then Pliable asked Christian this:
"Your book, is it all true?
Since, leaving much, I wish to have
A certainty in view."

2

"My friend, it's true," then Christian said;
  "Yes, very sure am I,
Because this book was made by One
  Who will not, cannot, lie."

"Since it is true," said Pliable,
  "What things are written there,
That make your heart so much rejoice,
  While on the way you are?"

He told of a kingdom where Jesus is king,
Where death has no power, is robbed of his sting;
A life that's eternal for all who get there,
And glorious crowns for his subjects to wear;
Of bright-shining garments that shine as the sun,
Which on arrival they'll give to each one;
No sorrow nor crying, he said, would be there,
No, nothing to call for a sigh or a tear.
He said that Cherubim, Seraphim, there,
Will dazzle our eyes to see as they are;
That thousands and thousands have gone there before,
And we shall behold them when we land on that shore,
All holy and harmless, the children of God,
Made so by the merits of Immanuel's blood.
He told of the Elders, how each had a crown,
Of all the good Martyrs who laid their lives down;
He said though their flesh had been burned in the flame,
They all were together and living again.

Said Pliable, "To hear of this
  Makes my heart overflow;
But how to have a share in it
  Is something yet to know."

Said Christian, " This is in my book,
  As plain as words can speak :
The governor of the place hath said
  That all shall have who seek.

" This offer now is made to all
  Who have a willing mind,
Who for the sake of heavenly things
  Forsake things earthly-kind."

Then Pliable to Christian said,
  " Come, let us mend our pace :
How glad I am to have the hope
  Of reaching such a place !"

Then Christian said, " How glad I'd be
  To speed along the road !
But go I cannot as I would ;
  See on my back this load."

Their conversation having ceased,
  They grew unwatchful now,
And near the middle of the plain
  They both fell in a slough.

The slough that they had fallen in
  I can explain in brief :
)espond is the sad name it bears ;
  It stands for unbelief.

Now Pliable was much perplexed
  By reason of the slough :
I heard him ask, with timid voice,
  " Where, Christian, are we now ?"

Now Christian made the sad reply,
  "I truly do not know."
Then Pliable offended was,
  And did quite angry grow.

" Is this the happiness," said he,
  " Of which I heard you speak?
So much ill luck as this at first,
  We worse things yet may meet.

" May I get out again with life,
  You may possess for me
All that great country, sir, alone;
  For there I'll never be."

Now, as he spake, he made a leap,
  Which took him from the slough:
Mark well, though he the bank had gained,
  'Twas next his own house now.

Away he went,—got out of sight;
  Him Christian saw no more;
He spent but very little time
  Before he reached his door.

Then Christian he was left to work
  In this great slough alone;
But still he strove to gain the side
  The farthest from his home.

He had a burden on his back,
  As I have said before:
This hindered him from getting out;
  It sank him down the more.

A man, whose name was Help, drew nigh,
  As I saw in my dream,
Who said, " What are you doing here,
  And how have you got in ?"

Said Christian, " One Evangelist
  Hath bade me go this way
To yonder gate, to save from wrath
  That will abide for aye.

" While running on to reach that gate,
  I was so filled with fear
That I the way did not see well ;
  And so I fell in here."

Help asked him why he had not looked,
  That he the steps might find.
Then Christian said, " I thoughtless was,
  So troubled was my mind."

Now Christian, by the hand of Help,
  Was drawn from miry clay ;
Help set him on good ground again,
  And bade him go his way.

Then I stepped up to him whose hand
  Had lifted Christian out:
I said, " This plat why not make good :
  It is the only route.

" No other way can travellers go
  To yonder gate, I'm sure,
But over this most dangerous plat :
  Why not have it secure ?"

He said to me, "This miry slough
    Can never be made good;
For if it had been possible,
    It would not long have stood.

"This place, dear sir, has chanced to be
    Where all the scum of sin
And filth that from conviction flow
    Do constantly run in.

"For when the sinner is awake,
    And sees his ruined state,
He thinks for him the die is cast,
    That now it is too late.

"This is the reason why this place
    Received the name it did:
The spirit of despondency
    The Scriptures do forbid.

"Some think this place remaineth bad
    By sanction of the King;
But I have seen enough myself
    To know it's no such thing.

"His laborers have been employed
    For eighteen hundred years
About this very miry place,
    But yet Despond appears.

"The very best materials
    Have in this place been cast,
Instructions by the wagon-load,
    And what is it at last?

" 'Tis true, the giver of the Law
  Has ordered steps secure,
Well planted through the midst of it,
  To make the footing sure.

" But there are seasons in the year
  It spews out mud and mire;
And then the steps are hardly seen,
  Though they are firmly there.

" And even when the steps are seen,
  Men often step aside;
Those subject to a dizzy head
  Get well with mud supplied.

" But, having entered by the gate
  Through this part of the road,
The footman finds a sweet relief,
  Because the ground is good."

I in my dream saw Pliable
  By this time had got home.
As soon as he was in the house,
  It all abroad was known.

His neighbors then came flocking in,
  That they might hear him tell
What he had seen while on the way,
  And what him had befell.

Some called him wise for coming back,
  But others called him fool;
And some set up to mock at him,
  And called him timid soul.

Said one, " Had I the venture made,
  I wouldn't have been so slack
As, for a few hard things at first,
  To come a coward back."

So Pliable felt quite alone,
  Looked foolish in the crowd ;
While all the rest were in a chat,
  He scarce dared speak aloud.

He soon regained his confidence ;
  His case was set aside ;
No time was lost, they all began
  Poor Christian to deride :

Now, Christian, who was in the fields,
  And walking quite alone,
Espied a man approaching him
  As yet to him unknown.

The space between them shorter grew ;
  At length they chanced to meet ;
And when they met, they had a talk
  Out in the open street.

The gentleman whom Christian met,
  While crossing o'er the way,
Was Worldly-Wiseman, from the town
  Of Carnal Policy.

The town of Carnal Policy
  Is great and flourishing,
And situated near the place
  Where Christian had lived in.

This man then meeting Christian did
   Him somewhat know, you see;
For such a setting out as his
   Could not a secret be.

His sighs and groans—yes, every move—
   Had made such public talk,
That any man along the way
   Could know him by his walk.

To Christian Worldly-Wiseman said,
   " Where bound with such a load?
I think your manner plainly tells
   You little know the road."

" A heavy load," then Christian said,
   " As ever creature had:
I'm sure when I get rid of it
   I shall be very glad.

" The way I go is onward, sir,
   To yonder little gate:
I there shall be put in the way
   To rid me of this weight."

Said Worldly-Wiseman to the man,
   " Since you are here alone,
Have you a wife, and children too,
   Whom you have left at home?"

" I have a wife, and children too;
   But them I don't enjoy,
This heavy burden on my back
   Does me so much annoy.

"Methinks I am as if I had
    No family at all;
Since they will not go with me now,
    I must forsake them all."

Said Worldly-Wiseman then to him,
    "Now hearken unto me:
I have extensive knowledge gained,
    And I can counsel thee."

"I'll hear good counsel," Christian said:
    "With it, kind sir, proceed:
Pressed like a cart beneath its sheaves,
    Good counsel I much need."

Then Worldly-Wiseman thus advised:—
    "In haste get off thy load,
For till thou dost, thou never canst
    Enjoy the gifts of God."

Said Christian, "That I wish to do;
    But I some help yet lack;
For no man in our country, sir,
    Can take it off my back.

"I cannot take it off myself;
    Now, this I plainly see:
I'm going, therefore, in this way,
    To have it done for me."

Then Worldly-Wiseman said to him,
    "Who sent thee on this road,
To seek some one who has the skill
    To rid thee of thy load?"

"A man," said Christian, "that appeared
  In honor to excel:
His name it was Evangelist,
  I do remember well."

Said Worldly-Wiseman, "I beshrew
  Him for his counsel given:
That way is the most dangerous
  That's found this side of heaven.

"This you will find, if you proceed
  As that man doth direct.
I see on you dirt from the slough:
  This might one well expect.

"But that deep slough is only where
  Their sorrows do begin
Who venture on this snareful way
  That thou art walking in.

"Hear me, an older man than thou;
  Hear what thou yet mayst meet:
Pain, hunger, perils, nakedness,
  And no chance for retreat.

"These things are true; they've been confirmed
  By many witnesses:
Swords, death, and darkness will, no doubt,
  Reward your carelessness."

Then Christian said, "This burden, sir,
  It me more terrifies
Than all the dangers of the way
  You've placed before mine eyes."

Then Worldly-Wiseman asked the man,
  "How came it on at first?
Of all that man is subject to,
  This burden is the worst."

"It came on me," then Christian said,
  "While reading in this book,—
This book of God, now in my hand,
  In which I daily look."

Said Worldly-Wiseman, "So I thought.
  Poor men of feeble mind,
By looking after things too high,
  Great difficulties find,

"Which do not only men unman,
  As thine, I see, have done,
But, to obtain they know not what,
  They desperate ventures run."

"I know," said Christian, "what I seek,—
  Ease from this heavy weight:
It lies upon me day and night,—
  This burden, oh, how great!"

Said Worldly-Wiseman, "Why seek ease
  In such a way as this,
Where dangers lurk along the path,
  And where no safety is?

"Now, I can point you out a way
  That leads to ease and friends,
A way at hand of pleasantness,
  Where danger ne'er attends."

"Keep not this secret," Christian said,
  "But open it to me,
That I may get this burden off,
  And I'll give thanks to thee."

"In yonder village," he replied,
  "Dwells one Legality;
The village, sir, in which he lives
  Is called Morality.

"This man maintains a noble name;
  He also hath the skill
Of taking burdens off like thine,
  Both when and where he will.

"Yea, to my knowledge he hath done
  No small amount of good,
By taking burdens off from men
  Who pass along that road.

"Besides, he hath the skill to cure
  Those somewhat crazy grown,
Who have by reason of their load .
  Been almost overcome.

"To him thou mayst in safety go;
  I'll venture this to say:
He will extend his help to thee,
  And that without delay.

"About a mile from where we stand,
  He and his son both dwell:
If he is not at home himself,
  His son will do as well.
                3

"When there, no doubt, thy burden can
    From thee be taken down;
Thy wife and children, too, be brought
    To dwell with thee in town.

"If thou back to thy native place
    Dost not desire to go,
(And I would not by any means
    Advise thee to do so,)

"There houses are unoccupied,
    And one that you can get;
I know that for a small amount
    Those houses will be let.

"Provisions, too, are kept on hand;
    The people are well clad;
And better neighbors to live by
    No man has ever had."

Now Christian halted for a while;
    But soon he did decide
To take the counsel of this man,
    And make his word his guide.

To Worldly-Wiseman Christian said,
    "Which way must I proceed
To find this good old honest man,
    In this my time of need?"

To Christian Worldly-Wiseman said,
    "Do you see yonder hill?"
"Yes," Christian then to Wiseman said,
    "I see it very well."

Said Worldly-Wiseman, "By that hill
   You go to where he lives;
The first nice house to which you come,
   When by the hill, is his."

So Christian to Legality
   Did turn his face to go
In search of help, and left the path
   Evangelist did show.

But now, behold, when Christian had
   This great hill got hard by,
He saw its sides hang o'er the way;
   'Twas also very high.

Now, Christian was afraid to walk,
   So overcome with dread
Lest this high hill, with all its rocks,
   Should fall upon his head.

Wherefore, a while he there stood still;
   His burden greater grew
Than it had been while in the way:
   He knew not what to do.

Great flames of fire also flashed
   From all sides of the hill,
Which made him fear he should be burnt
   Where he was standing still.

Here he began to quake with fear,
   And did so much perspire
That he was wet from head to feet
   While looking at the fire.

Now he grew very sorrowful
    That he had counsel taken
From Worldly-Wiseman, whom he met,
    And his own way forsaken.

Just then he saw Evangelist,
    Which filled him so with shame,
From holding down his head to blush
    He could no way refrain.

Evangelist came meeting him:
    As nigh he did advance,
He looked on trembling Christian now
    With dreadful countenance.

Evangelist then spake to him
    Without the least delay:—
"What, Christian, are you doing here?"
    Evangelist did say.

No answer did poor Christian make:
    He did not say a word,
But stood before him speechless now,
    As if he had not heard.

Now to investigate his case
    Evangelist began:—
" I found one crying in the street:
    Sir, art not thou the man?

" The city of Destruction, sir,
    I then was passing by;
I found a man without the walls
    Who like a child did cry."

Said Christian to Evangelist,
  "That weeping man was I:
This heavy burden on my back
  Was what then made me cry."

Evangelist to Christian said,
  "You'll find the way is straight;
Did I not put thee in the way
  To find the little gate?"

Said Christian to Evangelist,
  "I must confess you did;
My conscience says, Speak out the truth,
  Try not to keep it hid."

Evangelist then Christian asked,
  "How didst thou get astray,
So quickly get thee turned aside?—
  Thou art not in the way."

"As soon as I was through the slough,"
  Poor Christian to him said,
"A gentleman I chanced to meet
  Who did me thus persuade:

"That in the village I might find
  A very skilful man,
That soon could take my burden off:
  So towards it I ran."

Evangelist then further said,
  "This stranger, who is he
Who hath persuaded thee aside—
  This man, what can he be?"

3*

Said Christian, " Like a gentleman
    To me he did appear,
Talked much to me, got me to yield;
    I therefore now am here.

" But when I saw this awful hill,
    Position, height, and all,
I suddenly came to a stand,
    Lest it should on me fall."

Evangelist then asked him what
    That gentleman had said
When in the way he met with him,
    And how he was betrayed.

Then Christian said, " He asked me where
    I had set out to go ;
I frankly spake my mind to him,
    And gave him all to know."

Evangelist to Christian said,
    " What did he ask thee next?
I think there's been no little talk,
    Thou seemest so perplext."

Said Christian, "Then he asked me if
    I had a family.
I told him that I had, but they
    No comfort were to me:

" Because (said I) this burden does
    My comfort so destroy,
That I cannot my family,
    As formerly, enjoy."

" Now, Christian," said Evangelist,
   "What further did he say,
That all my kind directions thou
   So soon didst cast away?"

Said Christian, " He looked pitiful,
   And then with me did plead
That I would get my burden off,
   And get it off with speed.

" Ease from my burden, I told him,
   Is what I long have sought,
With sighs and groans and bitter tears,
   But I have found it not.

" I said, I'll go to yonder gate
   With my great burden on :
If there I fail to hear of help,
   I'll be the only one.

" But this man said that he to me
   A better way could show
Than that rough way you set me in,
   And bade me onward go.

" This way, said he, will lead you to
   A house where one doth dwell
Who can take burdens off like thine,
   And do it very well.

" Then I believed in what he said,
   And left your way for his,
With hopes to get my burden off;
   But I have done amiss.

" But when I came unto this place,
  And saw how things are here,
I stopped; I knew not what to do,
  I was so filled with fear."

Evangelist to Christian said,
  " Do thou a while stand still:
I'll show to thee the work of God
  Before we leave the hill."

So he to hear Evangelist
  Before him trembling stood;
He knew those words would blast his hopes,
  Or bring about his good.

Evangelist began to speak,
  And thus I heard him say:—
" Refuse not him that speaketh now,
  Nor dare to disobey;

" For if they have made no escape
  Who have rejected him
Who spoke to them while here on earth,
  What danger are we in

" If we presume to turn away
  From Him that speaks from heaven!
For this must be a greater sin,
  And may not be forgiven.

" Now, by their faith the just shall live,
  By faith, and not by sight;
But in the man that draweth back
  The Lord hath no delight."

Evangelist to Christian now
    Those words did thus apply:
"Thou art beginning to reject
    The words of the Most High,

"And from the only way of peace
    Thou hast begun to stroll:
Dear sir, thou art now hazarding
    The welfare of thy soul."

Then Christian fell before his feet,
    Like one whose life was gone,
And, as he fell, cried, "Woe is me!
    For I'm a man undone."

Evangelist then caught his hand,
    And said to him, "Believe!"
And told him, too, what numerous sins
    The Saviour can forgive.

Then Christian did somewhat revive,
    But trembled as at first,
While thus Evangelist to him
    The words of God rehearsed.

To Christian said Evangelist,
    As he did still proceed,
"To those things I shall tell thee of,
    Give thou more earnest heed.

"Now who it was deluded thee,
    Dear Christian, I will show;
Also the man whose praise he spoke,
    To whom he bade thee go.

" One Worldly-Wiseman,—he's the man
    'Twas thy bad luck to meet;
He loves the doctrine of this world,—
    He's tare among the wheat.

" To him the doctrine of the world
    Is gold without the dross ;
It suits the carnal mind the best,—
    It saves him from the cross.

" This man in spiritual things
    Doth never take delight,
But seeketh to pervert my ways,
    Although my ways are right.

" Three things in this man's counsel thou
    Must utterly abhor :—
His turning thee from the straight way,
    Thus causing thee to err ;

" His laboring the cross to make
    So odious to thee;
His setting thee in that broad way
    That leads to misery.

" Thou must abhor his turning thee
    Out of the better way;
Also thine own consenting to
    My words to disobey.

" For this alone is to reject
    The counsel of the Lord :
Do, therefore, not be governed by
    This Worldly-Wiseman's word.

"The Lord says, Strive to enter in,
  And that at the straight gate;
The gate that I shall send thee to,
  For that alone is straight.

"Straight is the gate that leads to life,
  And very few are they
Who enter by that narrow gate;
  But thousands go astray.

"Now, from this little narrow gate,
  And from the way thereto,
This man hath turned thee quite away:
  This soon would thee undo.

"His striving to make thee reject
  The Cross, thou must abhor:
It must be prized above the things
  That in all Egypt are.

"Besides, the King of Glory saith—
  Now, on his word rely—
That he who seeks his life to save,
  The same shall surely die.

"He that will love his friends or life
  In preference to me—
Them not comparatively hate—
  Can't my disciple be.

"This doctrine, too, thou must abhor,
  That that shall be thy death
Without which, Bible truth doth say,
  Eternal life none hath.

"Thou, too, must hate his setting thee
  Into the way of death:
His sending thee to whom he did
  Was but deceitful breath.

"The man to whom thou hast been sent
  Legality by name,
Is son to the bondwoman, who
  In bondage doth remain.

"Her children are in bondage too,
  And she, in mystery,
This very mountain Sinai is,
  That nigh had fell on thee.

"Now, if her children and herself
  In bondage still must be,
How canst thou, then, with reason hope
  By them to be made free?

"Therefore Legality cannot
  Set men from burdens free;
There's not a man he has relieved,
  Nor will there ever be.

"Now, ye cannot be justified
  By working for the Law;
For by its deeds no living man
  His burden can withdraw.

"This Wiseman, sir, an alien is,
  Legality's a cheat;
As for his son Civility,
  He's but a hypocrite.

"There's nothing now in all the noise
    These sottish men have made,
But a design to ruin thee,
    In all that they have said,

" By turning thee out of the way
    In which I thee had set:
Now think how foolish thou hast been,
    Thus taken in their net."

Evangelist then called aloud
    To Heaven to confirm
What he had said, that Christian might
    Another lesson learn.

And now came words and fire forth
    From the great towering hill
Beneath which this poor Christian stood:
    This caused his blood to chill.

These words Evangelist pronounced :—
    " All who work for the Law
Are under the most fearful curse,
    Can hence no comfort draw.

" For cursed are they, it written is,
    They who continue not
In all things written in the Law,
    To do them every jot."

Now Christian looked for certain death,
    Began to cry and fret;
He even cursed the time in which
    He Worldly-Wiseman met.

4

He said, " How foolish I have been,
    To hearken to his voice,
Whose arguments flow from the flesh !
    I've made a foolish choice."

He said then to Evangelist,
    "What think you of my state?
May I go back, sir, even now,
    Up to the little gate?

"Shall I not be abandoned there?
    For this sent back with shame?
I'm sorry I his counsel took:
    I am, no doubt, to blame.

" But may I be forgiven yet?
    Or is my sin too great?
Is mercy yet in store for me?
    Or is it now too late?"

Then said Evangelist to him,
    " Thy sin thou didst increase
By leaving for forbidden paths
    The only way of peace.

" But go to him who's at the gate;
    He yet will you receive;
He has much mercy for such ones,—
    He can their faults forgive.

" But now take heed unto thyself,
    And go no more astray;
Lest, when his wrath begins to burn,
    Thou perish from the way."

Then Christian did address himself,
  His journey back to take;
Evangelist gave him a kiss,
  Said, "Speed thee to the gate."

So he went on with haste, nor spake
  To any by the way:
If questions were proposed to him,
  He said not yea nor nay.

He went like one who all the while
  Treads on forbidden ground;
Nor could he feel himself secure
  Till he the right way found.

The time soon came when Christian reached
  The much-desired gate.
To see his duty, when once there,
  He had not long to wait;

For over it was written, "Knock!
  I'll open unto thee."
He knocked, and knocked, and knocked again,
  And thus I heard him say:—

"May I now enter here?　Will he within
  Open to sorry me, though I have been
  An undeserving rebel?　Then shall I
  Not fail to sing his lasting praise on high."

A grave-faced man came to the gate,
  Who was Goodwill by name:
He asked, "Who's here, what he would have,
  Also from whence he came."

Said Christian, "I'm a burdened man,
  And one that's prone to sin:
Since this way leads to Zion's gate,
  I pray thee, let me in.

"My native city I have left,
  Her dreadful end to shun:
My face I have set Zion-ward,
  I fear the wrath to come."

"I'll let you in, with all my heart,"
  To Christian said Goodwill:
Then open wide he threw the gate
  That leads to Zion's hill.

When Christian was just going in,
  The other to him said,
While giving him a gentle pull,
  "There's something now to dread.

"A little distance from this place
  There is a castle strong,
The captain's name Beelzebub:
  To him it doth belong.

"Now he, and they who with him are,
  Shoot arrows not a few,
To try to kill all those who seek
  This gate to enter through."

"Now I rejoice and tremble too,"
  Said Christian, when he thought
Of passing where Beelzebub
  With other men had fought.

Then said the man who kept the gate,
  To Christian, when safe in,
" Who hath directed thee this way?
  Pray, who so wise hath been?"

Said Christian, " One Evangelist
  Hath bade me come and knock :
He said my duty would be plain
  When I would hear thee talk."

Said Goodwill, " Sir, I see your face
  Is Zion-ward : to those
An open door is always set,
  No man can ever close."

Said Christian, " I begin to reap
  The benefits that rise
From running into hazards, sir,
  In this great enterprise."

Then Goodwill said, " How does it come
  That you have come alone?
'Tis said in time of danger two
  Are better far than one."

Said Christian, " I my danger saw ;
  My neighbors saw not theirs :
I therefore came this way alone,
  And well it with me fares."

Said Goodwill, " Of your coming here
  Did any of them know?
And did you warn them of their doom,
  A dreadful overthrow?"

4*

Then Christian said, "I told my wife,
  And all my neighbors, too;
But they did not regard my words:
  'Tis sad, but yet it's true.

"I was opposed on every side:
  They cried to me, Return!
My wife would not come with me here,
  So she is left to mourn."

"Did no one follow after you?"
  To Christian Goodwill said;
"To try to get you to return,
  Did not they you persuade?"

"Yes, Obstinate and Pliable;
  But they could not prevail:
Soon Obstinate gave me the back,
  And then began to rail.

"But Pliable from Obstinate
  Did differ, now you see:
He went not back just at that time,
  But came some way with me."

Then Goodwill said, "Since Pliable
  Did come a while with you,
Where is he now? why has he failed
  To come the journey through?"

"We came together," Christian said,
  "While all was going well;
But on the way there is a slough,
  And into it we fell.

"Here my poor neighbor Pliable
  Let all his courage fail,
Got out, but next to his own house,
  And thus began to rail :—

"Now, this brave place you so extol,
  You may possess for me;
And I'll go back to what I have,
  And leave it all to thee.

"So Pliable forsook me too,
  As now I do relate;
Went back to Obstinate again,
  While I came to this gate."

Then Goodwill said, "Alas, poor man!
  Is glory in his eyes,
Celestial glory, little worth,
  By him esteemed no prize,

"That he will not, in view of it,
  Small difficulties bear,
When he might soon, yes, very soon,
  Celestial glory share?"

Said Christian, "I of Pliable
  Have spoken truth indeed,
But might have spoken of myself
  And much the same have said.

"True, he went back to his own house
  And that with railing breath;
But also I had turned aside,
  To go the way of death,

" Persuaded by the arguments
    Of one whose words were fair,
One carnal Worldly-Wiseman, sir,
    A man of talent rare."

"So Worldly-Wiseman," Goodwill said,
    " Hath bade thee seek for ease
From old Legality, the cheat,
    The rogue, sir, if you please.

" No doubt they both are cunning cheats,
    And always wide awake.
Since he his counsel gave so free,
    Did you his counsel take?"

" Yes," Christian said, " far as I dare.
    Legality I sought,
Till, fearing that the hill would fall
    On all the place about,

" That hill, or mountain, near his house,
    Did fill me so with dread,
I saw no way that it could fail
    To fall upon my head."

" That mountain," Goodwill said, " has slain
    Its thousands, and may more:
'Tis well that you did there escape:
    It was from death's dark door."

Said Christian, " I can scarcely tell
    What might have been my fate,
Had not Evangelist met me
    Before it was too late.

" 'Twas through God's mercy that he came
   To wretched me again,
Or I, instead of being here,
   Had perished with the slain.

" But now I come, such as I am,
   Deserving more of death,
Than conversation with my Lord,
   Whose honor I address.

" But what a favor this to me,
   That I'm admitted here,
And find a hearty welcome, too,
   That drives away all fear!"

" All that will come, can enter here;
   They need not stand in doubt:
Though sinners once of crimson dye,
   We no wise cast them out.

" Therefore, good Christian, come with me,
   I'll teach thee of the way,
The narrow way that leads aright;
   All others lead astray.

" It was cast up by Patriarchs,
   By Prophets, and by Christ,—
The straightest and the safest way
   That ever was devised."

But Christian said, " May there not be
   Some windings in the way,
By which a stranger may get off,
   And somehow go astray?"

"Yes: many ways fall in with this,
    The crooked and the wide;
The right way, though, is always straight:
    Take this, sir, as a guide."

Now, in my dream I Christian saw
    Imploring him for aid:
"Oh, take this heavy burden down,
    That's on my back," he said.

As yet he was not rid of it,—
    That load of ponderous weight,—
Nor could he get it off alone,
    The burden was so great.

Said Goodwill, "Be content to bear
    Thy burden in this case:
It will fall off thy back itself,
    When at the proper place."

Then Christian girded up his loins,
    Gave hand, and bade farewell;
Then Goodwill said, "Some ways beyond,
    Interpreter doth dwell."

He said, "Go to the door and knock:
    That good man's always there,
And, being an Interpreter,
    He shows things great and rare.'

Then Christian, after taking leave,
    Made haste to reach his door:
When there, no one bade him come in
    Till he knocked o'er and o'er.

Then came one to the door, who said,
   "What man is this, I pray,
Who hath been knocking for some time,
   And hath not gone his way?"

Said Christian, "I'm a traveller,
   Bade call a while with you,
And with the master of the house
   To have an interview.

" By one of his acquaintances
   I have been bid to call,
That I may profit by this man
   Throughout my journey all."

The master of the house was called,
   Who did of him inquire
From whence he came, where he was bound,
   And what was his desire.

"The city of Destruction, sir,"
   Said Christian, " I am from :
I'm going to Mount Zion now,
   For my abiding home.

" Your neighbor, yonder, at the gate
   That heads the way, you see,
Told me to call,—that you could show
   Things that would profit me."

"Come in," said the Interpreter,
   " Come in, that I may show
Things that will be a help to thee
   Thy toilsome journey through."

Commanded he his man to bring
  A light without delay;
So Christian followed after him—
  The master led the way.

He took him to a private room;
  His man unlocked the door;
Then Christian saw some things, no doubt,
  He never saw before.

While sitting in the room, he saw
  A picture on the wall,
The likeness of a quite grave man,
  Eyes lifted up withal.

Its eyes were raised like one that looks
  Far up above his head;
The best of books was in its hand
  That man has ever read.

The law of truth was on its lips,
  A law that could be read;
The world was placed behind its back,—
  A crown above its head.

It stood erect upon its feet,
  As if with men it plead:
To him this silent orator
  Was eloquent, he said.

Said he to the Interpreter,
  "What meaneth what I've seen?
This picture hanging on the wall
  Must truly something mean."

" The man this picture represents
    Is of a thousand, one;
For few look up to things above,
    And few shall wear the crown.

" Whereas thou seest in its hand
    The best of books doth lie:
The law of truth, too, on its lips,
    Also its upward eye:

" It is to show his work is this,—
    To know and to unfold
Dark things to sinners, which have been
    Dark things to some of old.

" Whereas thou seest him standing up,
    As if with man to plead,
This aids in confirmation of
    What I before have said.

" The world is cast behind his back,
    Above him hangs a crown :
These show this world is not his home,
    He seeketh not renown.

" He thinketh light of present things,
    Through love to serve his Lord:
Great glory in the world to come
    Shall be his large reward.

" Now," said the good Interpreter,
    " The first of all beside,
I've showed the picture of the man
    Whom thou must take as guide.

5

"No other has been authorized
  By Zion's Lord and King:
Through places dark and difficult
  He can thee safely bring.

"And, now, to what I thee have showed
  Take thou most earnest heed;
All treasure up within thy heart
  Against the day of need,

"Lest in thy journey thou shouldst meet
  With some who may pretend
To lead thee right; when, oh! their path
  In misery shall end."

Interpreter then took his hand,
  And led him where was kept
A large and dusty parlor, that
  Had never yet been swept.

When Christian had reviewed a while,
  A man was called to sweep:
The dust then flew about so much
  He scarce his breath could keep.

To a young damsel who stood by,
  Interpreter then said,
"Bring water here, and sprinkle on,
  And let the dust be laid."

When this was brought and sprinkled on,
  Though all was dust before,
The room was cleansed with perfect ease,
  Wall, ceiling, and the floor.

Then Christian said, " What meaneth this,
   The parlor I have seen,
So full of dust, and never swept?
   This, too, must something mean."

" This represents the heart of man
   Unsanctified from sin :
The dust that flies about the room,
   What evils lurk within.

" The Law began to sweep, at first,
   Which made the dust to fly :
The Gospel brought the water in,
   Which made it all to lie.

" Whereas thou sawest, when the first
   Began to sweep, that he
Did raise the dust about the room,
   Which came nigh choking thee,

" This is to show the Law, instead
   Of cleansing one from sin,
Doth but revive it in the soul,
   And put more strength therein.

" The Law discovers and forbids
   All kinds of sin, 'tis true ;
But in its power lieth not
   The weakest to subdue.

" The damsel who the water brought,
   And laid the dust to rest,
Is like the blessed gospel to
   The sorrow-stricken breast.

"Its living waters purify,
  And lay the passions still;
It makes the heart a fount of joy,
  Which living waters fill.

"By it the heart is purified
  That once was full of sin,
And made a habitation for
  The everlasting King."

He took him in another room,
  And this he saw when there:—
Two little children, as they sat,
  Each in his little chair.

Now, Passion discontented was,
  Was often heard complain;
But Patience was a quiet child—
  This gave to him his name.

"What aileth Passion," Christian said,
  "That makes him discontent?
The younger child is not like him:
  Its time is sweetly spent."

"This Passion," said Interpreter,
  "Wants all his best things now:
His gov'nor wishes him to wait,
  And will not this allow.

"He wishes them to wait, he says,
  Till enters in next year:
Patience is willing and resigned,
  But Passion will not hear."

I saw one come to Passion then,
  Who had a bag of treasure,
And pour it down at Passion's feet,
  Who took it up with pleasure.

And, as he took it up, he laughed
  That Patience had to wait;
But soon he lavished all away,
  Made poverty his fate.

They all had gone, his treasures all
  Themselves made wings to fly;
I saw him last all clothed in rags,
  And with a downcast eye.

Said Christian to Interpreter,
  " Expound this unto me.
What meaneth these two little lads
  In this small room I see?"

Said he, " These lads are figures, and
  This, Passion, is to show
The feelings of those men whose hearts
  Are set on things below.

"This, Patience, is to represent
  Those who with patience wait
For their best things beyond this world
  And in a lasting state.

"I represent the present things
  Now by the present year,
The future by the year to come,
  Which is as yet not here.
                  5*

" Like Passion, some their portion want
   Now in the present year;
They say this waiting till the next
   May cost us very dear.

"With them this proverb is beloved,
   No better they could wish—
Give me the bird that's in the hand,
   For two that's in the bush.

" Whereas thou sawest how that he
   Soon wasted all his store,
Had nothing left at all but rags
   Of all he had before:

" So will it fare with all such men,
   Who have their good things here,
When this vain world has passed away,
   With all that they hold dear."

Said Christian, " Patience has, I think,
   Made much the wisest choice;
His things are incorruptible,
   In which he doth rejoice.

" 'Tis wise to wait with patience till
   He shall be clothed upon
With a white robe of righteousness,
   And with a golden crown.

" But foolish Passion shall have rags,
   A monument of shame,
For he has spent his substance all
   Fast as it to him came."

Now Passion did at Patience laugh,
  Because he waiteth long:
But Patience shall at Passion laugh,
  Whose things were first, but gone.

He that will have his portion first
  Will drink his fountain dry;
He that will have his portion last
  Will have it lastingly.

It, therefore, once of one was said:
  " Thy good things thou hast had:
Thou hadst them all in thy lifetime—
  How softly wast thou clad?

"But Lazarus—poor outcast man—
  Had only evil things:
But now he dwells with Seraphim,
  And with the King of Kings.

" And thou dost from thy doleful cell
  For water plead and cry;
Thy tongue shall be forever parched,
  Thy worm shall never die."

Then Christian said, " I now perceive,
  It is not best, like some,
To covet things that present are,
  But wait for things to come.

" 'Tis true, that things which now are seen
  Will soon have passed away,
But future things, yet out of sight,
  Will last through endless day.

" Though this be so, yet present things
   And fleshly appetite
Are to each other neighbours near,
   Therefore they do unite.

" But things to come and carnal sense
   Are strangers far apart,
And always so will they remain,
   Nor can be one in heart."

Now, in my dream, Interpreter
   Led Christian to a place
Where burned a fire on the wall,
   And rapid spread the blaze.

One stood by casting water on,
   The fire to subdue ;
But to accomplish this, he failed :
   The flame still hotter grew.

" Now he that cast the water on,
   To make the flame subside,
Is Satan—that old enemy :—
   His work shall not abide.

" Whereas thou seest that the flame
   Still upward doth ascend,
I'll show thee why the enemy
   Can't bring it to an end."

Interpreter then Christian led
   Away quite round the wall,
There stood a man who had with him
   A vessel full of oil.

This oil he secretly cast in
    Again, and yet again;
This is the reason he so well
    The fire can maintain.

Then Christian said, " What meaneth this,
    The fire in this place?"
" 'Tis Christ," Interpreter then said.
    " Christ with the oil of grace.

" With this he doth maintain the work
    When in the heart begun,
In spite of Satan's utmost rage,
    His people shall o'ercome.

" In that thou sawest him conceal'd
    Who kept the fire, doth show,
How grace is kept within the soul,
    This tempted scarcely know."

I also saw Interpreter
    Of Christian's hand take hold,
And lead him to a pleasant place—
    A palace to behold.

The palace was most beautiful,
    It Christian did delight;
When up thereto he had arrived
    Where all was plain in sight.

He also saw upon the top—
    Most beauteous to behold—
Some persons walking all about
    Arrayed in shining gold.

Then Christian asked Interpreter,
    " May we go in this place ?"
Interpreter then took his hand
    And led him on apace.

When Christian, by Interpreter,
    Was to the palace brought,
A company of men was there
    To enter, but dared not.

Now at this place there sat a man,
    A short space from the door,
This man sat at a table side,
    His ink-horn stood before.

He had a book to take the name
    Of every happy guest
Who had a right to enter in,
    And live among the blest.

He also saw in the door-way
    That men in armor stood,
To battle all that would go in,
    To wound them all they could.

Now Christian was somewhat amazed,
    He saw the men alarmed ;
And starting back for fear of those
    Who kept the door-way armed.

But soon he saw a man come up
    With a determined look,
Who said to him that sat to write,
    " Set my name in the book."

So when his name was written down,
    He, trusting in his Lord,
Then put a helmet on his head,
    And forthwith drew his sword.

When up to them he came, they laid
    On him with deadly force;
But he, with courage unimpaired,
    Pursued an onward course,

Now he began to cut and hack,
    And that most fiercely too,
Determined none should keep him out,
    The crowd he would go through.

When he had given many wounds,
    And often wounded been,
He cut his way through all the crowd,
    The palace entered in.

At this a very pleasant voice
    Was in the palace heard,
And all who walk'd about the top
    In the sweet chorus shared:

"Come in, come in,
    Eternal glory thou shalt win."

Now Christian in the palace went,
    And there was clothed as they.
"I think I know what this doth mean,"
    Did Christian smile and say.

"Now let me go," then Christian said;
    Interpreter said, "Stay!
I wish to show thee something more,
    Then thou shalt go thy way."

Into a room where all was dark
    He then did Christian take;
There sat one in an iron cage,
    This made his heart to ache.

The man was sad to look upon—
    He sat with downcast eyes,
His hands together folded were,
    He made heart-melting sighs.

"What meaneth this?" then Christian said;
    "Why is he in this place?"
"Ask him," said the Interpreter,
    "And learn his wretched case."

So Christian said: "Man, what art thou?"
    Then answered this poor man:
"I am not, sir, what I was once;
    I'll tell thee what I am.

"I once a bold professor was;
    Lord! Lord! I often cried,
And others often said of me
    That I was sanctified.

"For the Celestial City once
    I thought that I bid fair,
And even had most joyful thoughts
    About my getting there."

"What art thou now?" then Christian said,
  "If once so very fair."
"I am a man," he sighing said,
  "Shut up in keen despair;

"Like as this iron cage, it doth
  Encompass me about:
I am shut in on every side
  And never can get out."

"How camest thou," then Christian said,
  "Into this dreadful state;
Shut up as in this iron cage,
  Thy misery so great?"

"I ceased to watch and sober be,
  And to my lusts gave way;
I sinned against a loving God,
  'Twas thus I went astray.

"His precious word I did resist,
  Its light would not receive;
His Holy Spirit, it has fled—
  I did that Spirit grieve.

"I've tempted Satan, and he's come
  To keep me in this cage;
The holy God I have provoked
  To leave me to his rage.

"The most heart-melting truths I hear
  Will not make me relent;
I have so hardened my poor heart
  I never can repent."

6

Said Christian to Interpreter,
  " For such a man as this
Is there no hope, that after all
  He may attain to peace?"

" Ask him," said the Interpreter,
  Then Christian asked the man:—
" Is there no hope, but in despair:
  Must thou always remain?"

"No hope at all," then said the man;
  "This iron cage you see
Is such, that not one ray of hope
  Can ever dawn on me."

Said Christian : " Why, the Son of God
  Is pitiful and kind ;
Look up to him—his mercy plead,
  And leave thy fears behind."

" I've crucified," then said the man,
  "The Son of God afresh ;
I have his person, too, despised—
  Disdained his righteousness.

" I too have looked upon his blood
  As an unholy thing ;
Against the Spirit of his grace
  Did all my malice bring.

"By this, of all the promises,
  I am shut out, you see:
So nothing now at all remains.
  But threatenings to me:

"Dreadful threatenings—fearful ones,
  Of judgment just at hand,
And fiery indignation which
  I can no way withstand."

"For what," said Christian, "did you bring
  Yourself to this despair?
I would not for ten thousand worlds,
  Oh man! be where you are."

Said he: "The pleasures of this world
  I thought I should enjoy;
And promised to myself delight,
  With nothing to annoy:

"But now those things I once so loved
  Each bite me in their turn,
And do my very vitals gnaw,
  As would a living worm."

"But canst thou not repent and turn?"
  Then Christian kindly said.
"The Lord repentance hath withheld,"
  The woe-worn prisoner plead.

"His word gives no encouragement
  That will my fears assuage;
His own strong hand hath shut me up
  In this great iron cage.

"Not all the men that dwell on earth
  Can ever set me free;
Eternity, Eternity,
  Oh! dread Eternity!

"How shall I grapple with the pain
    That is awaiting me—
The vengeance of an angry God
    Throughout eternity."

Interpreter to Christian said,
    "Let this man's misery
An everlasting caution to
    Thyself, oh Christian, be."

Said Christian, "Fearful is this case;
    Oh God, help me to pray,
And watch, and sober be, that I
    May not thus go astray."

Said Christian to Interpreter,
    "I on my way must go."
"Nay, tarry," said Interpreter,
    "Till one thing more I show.

He then took Christian by the hand;
    Him to a chamber led,
Where he beheld a man who was
    Just rising out of bed.

And, as he put his garments on,
    He shook and trembled so,
That Christian asked Interpreter
    The reason why to show.

Interpreter then bade him tell
    To Christian why he shook;
When he awoke, and why he did
    So very fearful look.

So he began—to Christian said:
 "While in my sleep I dreamed
The heavens grew exceeding black,
 Like midnight gloom it seem'd:

"The lightnings blaz'd, the thunders roll'd
 Which filled my soul with dread;
The clouds did rack unusually
 That passed above my head.

"With this I heard a trumpet sound,
 The blast was long and loud;
I saw one coming down the skies,
 And seated on a cloud;

"Attended by the heavenly host,
 All in a burning flame,
The heavens too lit up with fire,
 Before them as they came.

"'Twas then I heard a voice proclaim
 With a tremendous sound:
'Arise ye dead, to judgment come,
 Ye nations under ground!'

"The solid rocks assunder rent:
 The graves gave up their dead:
Some looking up rejoiced aloud,
 While others shook with dread.

"Some in the anguish of their souls,
 Sought for a place to hide
Beneath the ruins of the world,
 They were so terrified.

6*

" The man who sat upon the cloud
    Then bade the world draw near;
Then from his book their sentence read,
    That each his doom might hear.

" Yet for the flames that issued forth
    And did the throne surround,
None any nearer could approach
    Than his appointed bound;

" Like as our earthly judges have,
    Where waiting prisoners are,
A distance separating them
    From prisoners at the bar.

" Said he to those attendants who
    Did round about him wait,
' Cast ye the stubble, tares, and chaff
    Into the Burning Lake.'

" With this just whereabout I stood
    Then opened wide the pit;
Great smoke and coals of fire with noise
    Burst from the mouth of it.

" He said to those who burned the tares,
    ' Go gather up my wheat;
It safe into my garner store,
    The time has come to reap.'

" With this I many saw caught up
    Away into the clouds;
But I, for one, was left behind
    Among the weeping crowds.

" I also sought myself to hide,
  But I could not, for He
That sat upon the clouds of heaven
  Still kept his eye on me.

" My sins came to my guilty mind ;
  My guilty conscience spake ;
This ended all my fearful dream,
  For then I came awake."

" But what was it," then Christian said.
  " That gave you such a fright,
That put you in an agony
  While gazing on the sight?"

" What put me in this agony ?"
  The man to Christian said,
" I thought the Judgment Day was come,
  My peace with God not made.

" But this affrighted me the most ;
  When I began to find
The angels gathered several,
  But me they left behind.

" And, also, then the pit of hell
  Did open where I stood.
My conscience then did me accuse,
  I knew I was not good.

" And, as I thought, the Judge's eyes
  Were always fixed on me ;
I thought I indignation in
  His countenance could see."

Interpreter to Christian said,
  " Of all that thou hast seen,
Hast thou well pondered in thy heart
  To know what they may mean ?"

Said Christian, " Yes: so that they have
  Put me in hope and fear;
The dark side lays my spirits low,
  The bright side doth me cheer."

" Remember," said Interpreter,
  " Those things I did thee show;
Let them like goads still prick thy sides,
  That thou may'st onward go."

Now he began to gird his loins
  His journey to pursue;
The other said, "The Comforter,
  Good Christian, be with you,

" To guide you to the city safe,
  Be with you on the way."
Then Christian ventured out again,
  And thus I heard him say :—

' Here have I seen things rare and profitable;
  Things pleasant, dreadful things, to make me stable
In what I have begun to take in hand;
  Then let me think on them, and understand
Wherefore they showed me here, and let me be
  Thankful, O good Interpreter to thee."

Now, in my dream I saw the way
    That Christian passed, and all
The highway fenced on either side:
    Salvation was its wall.

Now up this way, dear Christian ran,
    With difficulty great,
Because the burden on his back
    Was of distressing weight.

He ran till he came where there was
    Somewhat ascending ground:
Erected on that very spot,
    A wooden cross he found.

Below the cross, not far from it,
    A sepulchre was too,
Of these I had, while in my dream,
    A very pleasant view.

I saw, when Christian had come here,
    His burden rolled away;
Into the sepulchre it fell,
    Below the cross to stay.

This burden, which no strength on earth
    Could free him from before,
Fell off when at the cross and grave,
    And then was seen no more.

Then Christian glad and lightsome was,
    And said, with cheerful breath,
" Rest by His sorrow I have gained,
    And life, too, by His death."

He then a while stood still to look,
  And wondered how it was
That his great burden fell from him
  While looking at the cross.

He looked, therefore, and looked again,
  (As Zechariah speaks,)
Till all the springs within his head
  Sent water down his cheeks.

He, while thus weeping here for joy,
  Three shining ones did see,
Who came to him, saluted him
  With, " Peace be unto thee."

The first said, " Christian, though thy sins
  Where many, all are gone."
The second stripped him of his rags
  And put good raiment on.

The third then set a mark upon
  The forehead of this man,
Gave him a Roll with seal on it,
  To look on as he ran.

He told him he must give it in
  At the Celestial Gate.
These shining three then went their way,
  They did no longer wait.

Then Christian gave three leaps for joy,
  More happy than a king;
His heart, now full of gratitude,
  He thus began to sing :—

" Thus far did I come laden with my sin :
Nor could ought ease the grief that I was in,
Till I came hither.   What a place is this !
Must here be the beginning of my bliss ?

" Must here the burden fall from off my back ?
Must here the strings that bind them to me crack ?
Blessed cross ! blessed sepulchre ; blessed rather be
The man that there was put to shame for me !"

Isaiah lv. 6, 7.

Seek ye the Lord while he may be found, call
ye upon him while he is near :

Let the wicked forsake his way, and the un-
righteous man' his thoughts : and let him return
unto the Lord, and he will have mercy upon
him ; and to our God, for he will abundantly
pardon.

John iii. 16.

For God so loved the world, that he gave his
only begotten Son, that whosoever believeth in
him should not perish, but have everlasting life.

Matt. xi. 28.

Come unto me, all ye that labour and are
heavy laden, and I will give you rest.

MATT. vii. 13, 14.

Enter ye in at the strait gate: for wide *is* the gate, and broad *is* the way, that leadeth to destruction, and many there be which go in thereat:

Because strait is the gate, and narrow *is* the way, which leadeth unto life, and few there be that find it.

MATT. vii. 7.

Ask, and it shall be given you; seek, and ye shall find; knock, and it shall be opened unto you.

REV. xx. 11–15.

And I saw a great white throne, and him that sat on it, from whose face the earth and the heaven fled away; and there was found no place for them.

And I saw the dead, small and great, stand before God; and the books were opened: and another book was opened, which is *the book* of life: and the dead were judged out of those things which were written in the books, according to their works.

And the sea gave up the dead which were in it; and death and hell delivered up the dead which were in them: and they were judged every man according to their works.

And death and hell were cast into the lake of fire. This is the second death.

And whosoever was not found written in the book of life was cast into the lake of fire.